I LOVE SPRING

By Lizzie Scott and
Stephanie Fizer Coleman

Published in Canada
Crabtree Publishing
616 Welland Ave.
St. Catharines, Ontario
L2M 5V6

Published in the United States
Crabtree Publishing
347 Fifth Avenue
Suite 1402–145
New York, NY 10016

Published in 2021 by Crabtree Publishing Company

Printed in the U.S.A./122020/CG20201014

Words that are **bolded** are explained in the glossary on page 32.

Author: Lizzie Scott

Editorial director: Kathy Middleton

Editor: Sarah Peutrill

Designer: Lisa Peacock

Illustrator: Stephanie Fizer Coleman

Proofreader: Kathy Middleton

Production coordinator and Prepress technician: Margaret Amy Salter

Print coordinator: Katherine Berti

Library and Achives Canada Cataloguing in Publication

Title: I love spring / by Lizzie Scott and Stephanie Fizer Coleman.
Other titles: Spring
Names: Scott, Lizzie (Children's author), author. | Coleman, Stephanie Fizer, illustrator.
Description: Series statement: I love the seasons | Previously published under title: Spring. | Includes index.
Identifiers: Canadiana (print) 20200367234 | Canadiana (ebook) 20200367250 | ISBN 9781427129086 (hardcover) | ISBN 9781427129123 (softcover) | ISBN 9781427129161 (HTML)
Subjects: LCSH: Spring—Juvenile literature.
Classification: LCC QB637.5 .S36 2021 | DDC j508.2—dc23

Library of Congress Cataloging-in-Publication Data

Names: Scott, Lizzie (Children book author), author. | Coleman, Stephanie Fizer, illustrator.
Title: I love spring / by Lizzie Scott and Stephanie Fizer Coleman.
Description: New York : Crabtree Publishing Company, 2021. | Series: I love the seasons | First published in Great Britain in 2020 by The Watts Publishing Group.
Identifiers: LCCN 2020045668 (print) | LCCN 2020045669 (ebook) | ISBN 9781427129086 (hardcover) | ISBN 9781427129123 (paperback) | ISBN 9781427129161 (ebook)
Subjects: LCSH: Spring--Juvenile literature.
Classification: LCC QB637.5 .S423 2021 (print) | LCC QB637.5 (ebook) | DDC 508.2--dc23
LC record available at https://lccn.loc.gov/2020045668
LC ebook record available at https://lccn.loc.gov/2020045669

Contents

Thinking about spring 4
Spring weather 6
Sunshine and showers 8
Warm layers 10
Dressing for rain 12
Leaves and blossoms 14
The sounds of spring 16
Walks in the woods 18
Spring in the garden 20
Spring on the farm 22
New life 24
Nests and eggs 26
Spring celebrations 28
Looking forward to summer 30
Glossary and index 32

When I think of spring, I think of bright sunshine and fresh air. The cold of winter has gone. I can play outside without a heavy coat!

What makes you think of spring?

What kinds of flowers make you think about spring?

Spring is one of the seasons. The four seasons are spring, summer, fall, and winter. In spring, the Sun gets stronger and there are more hours of sunlight.

Spring is warmer than winter, but colder than summer. In spring, the Sun may feel warm, but the wind can be cold.

I like to fly my kite on windy days.

Have you ever flown a kite?

Springtime makes me think of sunshine and rain showers. Strong winds blow rain clouds quickly across the sky.

What are the best clothes to wear in windy weather?

Sometimes in spring it is rainy and sunny at the same time. Then you may see a rainbow in the sky.

Do you know the seven colors of a rainbow?

When the air is cold in spring, I wear clothes that will keep me warm. I wear long pants and a sweater or jacket.

The weather can change quickly in spring. It is a good idea to wear many layers of clothing.

On sunny spring days, I can play outside in a T-shirt. After the cold of winter, it is nice to feel the warm sunshine on my skin.

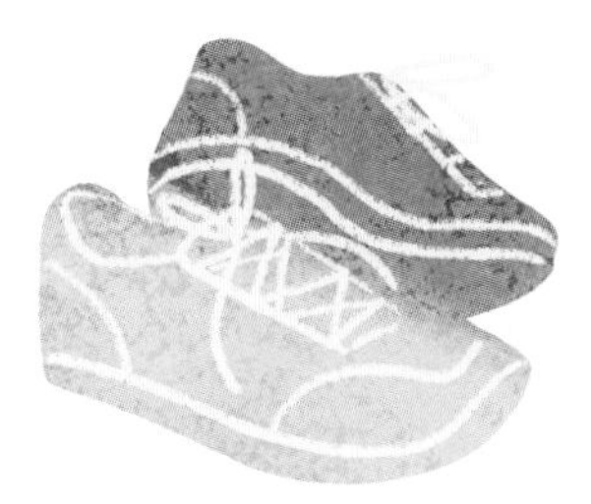

What clothes do you wear in spring?

I like to go for walks in spring. When I go outside in rainy weather, I wear a raincoat and rubber boots in case it rains.

I like to splash in puddles when I'm wearing my rubber boots.

Do you like to splash in puddles?

Have you seen trees covered in bright green leaves in spring? Some trees lose their leaves in the fall. In spring, the weather gets warmer. **Buds** open and new leaves appear.

Where do you see flowers blooming or **blossoms** on trees in spring?

I look forward to hearing the sounds of spring. The Sun rises early and so do the birds. Sometimes I can hear them singing at **dawn**, as soon as it gets light.

In spring, playgrounds are full of the sound of children having fun. I like to spend more time outside after the cold winter months have passed.

I like to go to the woods in spring. The leaves on the trees are young and small. Sunlight shines through the leaves to the ground.

In the woods, the air feels fresh. You can smell the sweet scent of spring in the air.

What is your favorite thing about walking in the woods in the springtime?

In spring, I like to plant lettuce in the garden. Spring is a good time of year for planting. The soil becomes warmer and plants grow quickly.

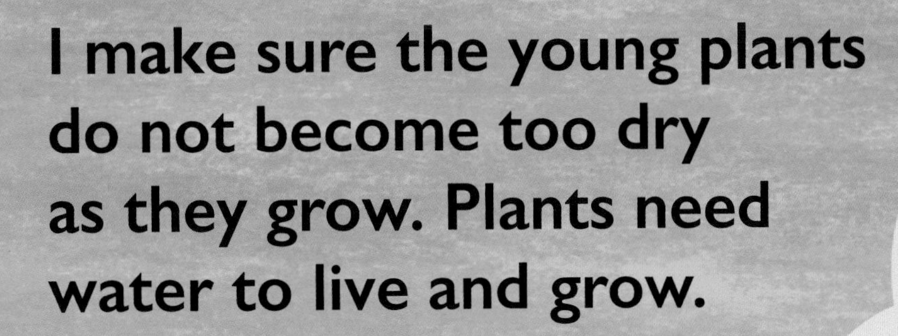

I make sure the young plants do not become too dry as they grow. Plants need water to live and grow.

What else do young plants need?

Have you ever visited a farm in spring?

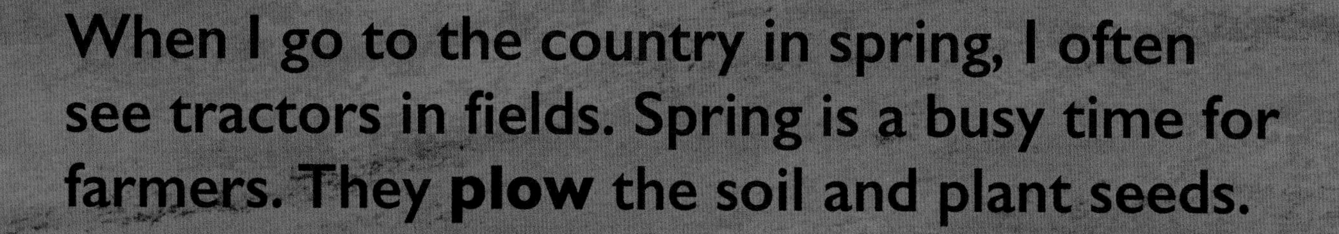

When I go to the country in spring, I often see tractors in fields. Spring is a busy time for farmers. They **plow** the soil and plant seeds.

Farmers sometimes use scarecrows in their fields. They protect the **crops** from hungry birds. The scarecrows are dressed in old clothes. Sometimes they are filled with straw.

How do you think a scarecrow helps to keep birds away?

Springtime makes me think of new life. Lots of animals are born at this time of year. On farms, sheep give birth to lambs and cows have calves.

In spring, sometimes you can see ducklings learning to swim.

What kind of food do you think ducks like to eat?

Sometimes I see birds collecting twigs and straw for nests.

Has a bird ever built a nest near your home?

Spring is also when birds lay their eggs.

If you see a bird's nest, why should you not touch the eggs?

Springtime makes me think of spring **celebrations**. All around the world people celebrate spring in different ways.

People paint eggs, gather at flower festivals, and watch parades.

They even have picnics under the spring trees!

As spring goes by, the days get longer and warmer. After the short days of winter, it's light enough again to walk home through the park after school.

What do you like doing after school in spring?

In late spring, hot days are not far away. I get out my shorts, and get ready for the fun days of summer!

Glossary

buds Small flowers that are not yet fully grown
blossoms Small fully grown flowers
celebrations Gatherings of people to mark a special event
crops Plants grown to be used for food or other uses
dawn Time of day when it starts to become light
plow To break up the soil before planting seeds

Index

air 4, 10, 19
animals 24, 25

birds 16, 23, 26-27
blossom 15, 29
buds 14

clothes 4, 8, 10-13, 31
crops 23

ducks 25

eggs 27, 28

farms 22-23, 24
festivals 28-29
flowers 5, 15, 28, 29

garden 20-21

kite 7

leaves 14, 18

nests 26-27

planting 20, 22
plants 20-21
playgrounds 17

rain 8-9, 12, 13
rainbow 9

scarecrow 23
school 30, 31
sounds 16-17
Sun 4, 5, 6, 8, 9, 11, 16, 18

trees 14-15, 18, 29

walks 12, 19, 30
weather 6-9, 10, 11, 12, 14, 30, 31
wind 6-7, 8
woods 18-19